CONFIRMATION NOTEBOOK

Confirmation Notebook

*A guide to
Christian belief and practice*

SIXTH EDITION

◆

Compiled by

Hugh Montefiore

First published in Great Britain in 1968 as *My Confirmation Notebook*
Fifth edition, revised and reset, published in 1984

Sixth edition, revised and reset, published in 2002 by
Society for Promoting Christian Knowledge
Holy Trinity Church
Marylebone Road
London NW1 4DU

British Library Cataloguing-in-Publication Data
A catalogue record for this book is available from the British Library

ISBN 0-281-05521-1

Designed and typeset by Kenneth Burnley, Wirral, Cheshire.
Printed in Great Britain by Bookmarque Ltd, Croydon, Surrey

Contents

CONTENTS

Introduction

This Notebook has been completely revised and is reissued with a modified title. It was originally written (in some haste) for confirmation classes nearly 35 years ago (and enlarged as successive liturgies were approved for use in the Church of England).

My aim remains the same as when it was first published. I wrote five editions back: 'It is a cardinal principle of this notebook that, whatever be the age of the confirmed, the notes themselves are written for adults in adult language.'

It can also be more broadly used. There are nowadays as many adults as adolescents preparing for confirmation. Adult study groups, as well as confirmation groups, and individuals who need short summaries of Christian belief and practice, will find the book helpful.

It is true that the process of adult learning takes place through a personal search for integrity and truth, and through 'whole person' mutual questioning within group discussions. For this very reason it is desirable, in my judgement, to have clear, succinct notes about the content of Christian belief.

The notes may also be given to younger candidates for confirmation so that, when they grow older, they may also possess adult notes on their Christian faith.

HUGH MONTEFIORE

1

The Reality of God

1 God revealed himself in Jesus as fully as human personality permits, so that we can know the nature of God in a personal way. Through Jesus we can all know God.

2 According to John 14.9 (AV), Jesus said: 'He that hath seen me hath seen the Father.' This implies that Jesus helps us to understand the reality of God. 'He that cometh to God must believe that he is, and that he is a rewarder of them that diligently seek him' (Hebrews 11.6 AV).

3 We cannot see God's inner nature, only his footsteps, his activity. 'No man hath seen God at any time' (John 1.18 AV). Definitions or descriptions of God can only point towards his reality. God is vaster than we can conceive, greater than we can imagine.

4 There is much that we can never know about God; but still, we can truly know him. Faith is the proper means by which we know God. This kind of knowledge is very different from scientific knowledge and rather different from, say, knowledge of people; but it is not in any sense an inferior way of knowing.

5 It is reasonable to believe in God since:

   (i) God reveals himself to us;

  (ii) we all experience God in our lives (although we may not recognize this as experience of God); and

 (iii) our minds tell us that it is more reasonable to believe in the reality of God than not.

6 Here are some of the reasons why our minds tell us that it's more reasonable to believe in God than not:

  (a) The world cries out for some reason why it exists and continues to exist. God alone supplies that reason.

  (b) Most people agree that the ideas of the good and of the beautiful and of the true are not just the result of their 'feelings'. This suggests that they are reflections of him who is Truth, Beauty and Goodness.

  (c) Human beings need God. God meets our deepest needs for affection, challenge and security, our 'immortal longings'. In the process of evolution, the development of a need suggests it can be met. Our need for God suggests that God must exist.

  (d) With the growth of scientific knowledge, many find that the spiritual and intellectual endowments of human beings, the beauty and complexity of the universe (in minute particles of matter as much as in the vastness of space), cannot be due just to chance, but are the result of God's providence.

  (e) We now know that there is much 'fine tuning' in the laws of nature without which the emergence of life would have been impossible.

7 The reasons for believing in the reality of God are not proofs: they are 'demonstrations' for those with eyes to see. We cannot 'prove' God's existence in the same way as we can prove that an object or a person exists. God is not only 'infinite', so that his existence is not in time and space; but also God contains the universe within himself, so that 'in him we live, and move, and have our being' (Acts 17.28 AV). If God is like that, of course he cannot be 'proved'.

8 Most people who believe in God don't believe for the reasons given above. They have been brought up to accept God on faith, and they have experienced him in their lives. He is 'the Beyond in their midst'.

9 Not all accept the reality of God. There are agnostics (not sure about God) and atheists (sure God doesn't exist). Usually they protest against our distorted views about God. Some people believe that science has 'disproved' religion. This is now rather old-fashioned. Certainly scientific knowledge is tested by doubt while religion operates by faith. But science is concerned with finding out how God's world has evolved and how it works. Religion on the other hand is concerned with our relationship with God. Many scientists are very religious people.

10 Although the limitations of language force us to use gender in talking about or talking to God, he is neither male nor female, nor is he impersonal. He is suprapersonal.

11 We experience God in many ways. Some people have a mystical or a conversion experience. Most people recognize God's footsteps in his created universe, and see God in what is true, good, and beautiful. They feel that Love has a reality outside themselves. They find in their lives an unconditional demand and grace. They feel strengthened by God's help; they feel traces of his plan working out in their lives. They find that God is brought near to them by Jesus, through worship and sacrament and private prayer.

12 No one can get God 'taped'. There is always far more about God that we don't know than we do know. Faith is mixed with doubt, and is not the same as certainty. Faith means trusting in God, opening your heart and mind to him, betting your life on him. We can rightly have a firm conviction and a living faith.

NOTES

2

God in the Modern World

1 Problems

We live in a world full of problems; evil and suffering, divisions and hatred (between classes, races, and sexes), the very rich and the very poor. There are problems of the environment, problems of power, even the power to annihilate whole peoples through nuclear war. How does the idea of God fit into this modern world?

2 Evil

God permits evil. His Son submitted to it on the cross, and by so doing he was victorious over its power to harm him. The origin of evil remains a mystery. But without the possibility of evil we could not choose the good. Christians believe that Christ has delivered them from falling under the power of evil. We mature and grow in character by refusing the evil and choosing the good. God leaves us free to choose, because he wants us to grow into his own perfect freedom. This freedom of choice, however, involves the possibility of people perpetrating great evil.

3 Suffering

Suffering is never to be desired for ourselves or for others. It can, however, lead us to experience a new depth of living and under-standing, although excessive pain can reduce us to mere self-awareness. Jesus revealed God's attitude towards suffering. In his healing ministry, he reduced suffering where he could. But he made no attempt to avoid suffering for himself when he was threatened by it.

4 Power

We live in a world where there are terrible abuses of power. In some countries there is torture, brainwashing, religious and political persecution, deliberate distortion of truth. Man's ingenuity has produced terrible armaments, and there is the ever-present threat of nuclear, chemical and biological war. These abuses of power are the result of humankind's choice of evil rather than good. They can only be remedied by a responsible use of power. Jesus contrasted the despotic use of power with that of his own lifestyle (Mark 10.41–5). Christians are not called to turn their back on power but to use it responsibly.

5 Powerlessness

In the modern world many feel powerless. They are caught, as it were, in a trap. They cannot contribute to decision-making. They cannot find employment. They cannot affect their own future. They feel stripped of self-esteem and deprived of human dignity. Jesus voluntarily allowed himself to be 'handed over' to the religious and secular authorities, and so he voluntarily shared this experience of powerlessness. By so doing he showed God's self-identification with the powerless.

6 Technology

Technology is the harnessing of scientific knowledge to practical use. It can be used for great good or for great evil. It has transformed the kind of life that we lead. It has reduced drudgery, increased consumption of goods, aided health, enabled mass communication and mass transport. At the same time it is likely to reduce paid employment (by automation), cause population explosion (by reducing infant mortality and extending life expectancy) and increase war risks (by sophisticated weapons systems). It is possible for machines to dominate us, instead of us controlling machines. We need to be responsible in the ends for which we use technology and in our choice of appropriate technology. God gave to human beings power and wisdom to use aright.

7 One World

God 'created every race of men of one stock, to inhabit the whole earth's surface' (Acts 17.26). We live in one world. Jesus said: 'You have the poor among you always' (Mark 14.7), but he showed special concern for the deprived. Today the Third World is greatly deprived compared with the rest of humankind. Its peoples die of hunger and disease, and suffer indignities of gross poverty. They need not merely first aid, but help to build up their own skills, capital and self-respect. Globalization shows us that we are all members of one world, but its practical effect is to make the rich countries richer and the poor ones poorer.

8 The Environment

The environment is subject to particular stress at the present time. A whole network of ecological problems is caused by population increases, by affluence, by technology, by under-regulated capitalism and by economic growth. Species are threatened and extinguished, non-renewable resources are becoming very greatly reduced, widespread pollution is caused, fertility of the soil is threatened or eroded, greenhouse gases are causing global warming. God gave human beings dominion over nature (Genesis 1.26). According to the story of the Garden of Eden,

Adam was placed in the garden to co-operate with nature, which was both intrinsically good and useful for people (Genesis 2.9, 15). God intended humankind to exercise proper stewardship over nature.

9 *The Family*

The family is the natural God-given unit in which human beings can find fulfilment and in which children can grow up in security to reach proper maturity. Today the family is in difficulties. Cheap and easily available contraceptives encourage premarital and extramarital sex. Nearly two-fifths of children are born outside marriage (in 2000). Lone parents form 22 per cent of all families (in 2001), with children lacking a role model of father or mother. Lack of parental discipline results in the loss of some children's sense of security. Working hours can cause some parents to lack time to give to their children. Unrealistic expectations and easy divorce are among the causes of the death of one out of three or four marriages. Mobility, the break-up of the extended family, and longer expectation of life increase family stresses. Jesus taught that the claims of God were greater than those of the family (Mark 3.35), but he took for granted the family unit, and spoke of God as his Father.

10 *God in the Modern World*

These are some of the problems of modern life. There is no easy solution to any of them. But God is relevant to all of them, and we are given clues about what should be our attitude to them, and how we should face them.

3

Why Confirmation?

1   To be a Christian means to follow in the way of our Lord Jesus Christ, with all that this entails. Creeds and conventions have their place, but neither are a substitute for perseverance in following the example of Jesus.

2   The Notes of this Christian Notebook will not make you a full Christian. Christianity is a way of life, not a matter of learning up facts and ideas. Nevertheless we owe it to God and to ourselves to try to understand the three sides of the Christian religion; that is:

  (i)   doctrine – what we believe;
 (ii)   duty – how we should behave; and
(iii)   devotion – worship and prayer.

3   *Scriptural Basis of Confirmation*

  (a)   *The Laying on of Hands*   is used in New Testament times for various purposes (healing, ordination, commissioning).

  (b)   *Confirmation*   was administered to Samaritans who had been baptized but who could not yet enjoy the Christian experience (Acts 8.17); and also to some Ephesians who had only known John's baptism (Acts 19.6).

  (c)   *Confirmation*   in the New Testament is a sign and symbol of strengthening, to enable people to enjoy and experience full membership of the Christian Church.

(d) *The New Testament* shows the origin of confirmation; but its function has changed with differing circumstances. Its use cannot be proved necessary, but it is a vital, symbolic, useful and meaningful part of the discipline of the Church of England. We need something outward to mark full membership of our Church.

4 *The Meaning of Confirmation*

This depends on whether a person (i) was christened as a baby but is unconfirmed, or (ii) is to be baptized as an adult, or (iii) is a full member of another Church, but is now joining the Church of England.

(i) *For Those Christened as Babies but Not Confirmed*
At its christening a child is made a member of Christ, as the word 'christen' implies. He or she is brought within the influence of the Church, and within the ambit of its prayers for God's help. The parents affirm their intention to bring up the child as a Christian and the godparents (the Church's representatives) witness to this. But when people grow up and are old enough to answer for themselves, they are no longer responsible for promises made by others. At confirmation these people publicly renew (or confirm) those promises and pray for God's grace to strengthen (or confirm) their life of Christian discipleship.

(ii) *For Those Baptized and Confirmed as Adults*
For adults, baptism and confirmation have a single meaning, and should take place at the same time. Baptism means identifying with Christ; 'drowning' under the waters and being raised to newness of life. This was the pattern of Jesus's life, and so of the Christian life within the Church. It means finding oneself through abandonment of self-concern and by reliance on God. Confirmation is a 'seal' marking the

completion of Christian initiation and full membership of the Church.

(iii) *For Full Members of Other Churches*

For these people confirmation means the transfer of allegiance from a protestant Church to the Church of England. This does not mean the denial of former blessings: it marks rather a decision to join the ongoing historic Church of this country, and to enter into its tradition. (Roman Catholics and Orthodox Christians joining the Church of England are not 're-confirmed' but 'received'.)

5 Our Promises

In the *Common Worship* service, there are decisions to be made:

 (i) to reject evil and to renounce sins;
(ii) to turn to Christ as Saviour and Lord, and as the way, the truth and the life.

Those being confirmed make (together with the congregation) a profession of the Christian faith in the words of the Nicene Creed. Preparation classes are held to help them to know what all this entails and to find support from one another.

6 God's Promises

The laying on of hands is a personal sign of God's promise given through Christ that he will care for us and give us grace to respond, through his Holy Spirit working within us. By opening ourselves to God, we allow the release of the Spirit to make us whole people, able to make a full response to God.

7 The Beginning, Not the End

At confirmation begins full membership of the Church, and this should mean active membership. It is like 'coming of age': it marks the start of a mature and responsible Christian life. From this time onwards the great privilege of sharing fully in the Holy Communion is given to the Christian.

8   *The Universal Church*

Confirmation entails the laying on of hands with prayer by a *bishop*. He personally represents the universal Church of Christendom, vertically down the ages and horizontally across the world. At confirmation people join fully in the life of their congregation, which is the local embodiment of the universal Church throughout the world.

NOTES

4

Jesus of Nazareth

1 *Jesus's Birth*   The stories of Jesus's birth (Matthew 1—2,
   Luke 1—2) are written to show:

   (i)   that God made a fresh start with Jesus;
   (ii) that Jesus fulfilled Jewish hopes;
   (iii) that Jesus was not only fully human, but also Son of God.
         (Jesus claimed this Sonship for himself, but he did not
         appeal to his birth to prove it.)

2 *Jesus's Mother*   Mary consented to be the mother of our Saviour
   (Luke 1.38). Without that consent, the incarnation could not
   have happened as it did. Mary was responsible for Jesus's
   upbringing as a child, so that his human nature must have been
   influenced by her. She is to be honoured because of her Son
   (Luke 1.42), but Jesus gave higher honour to doing the will of
   God (Luke 11.28).

3 *The Hidden Years*   For most of his life (until he was over 30) Jesus
   lived an ordinary obscure life, following the family trade at
   Nazareth. These 'hidden years' show:

   (i)   the great humility of God;
   (ii) that ordinary quiet lives can be pleasing to God;
   (iii) that it really is possible to live at home and at work without
         sin, for Jesus did.

4 **_The Ministry_** This lasted probably about three years. It starts with:

(a) *Baptism* Jesus was baptized (submerged in water) as one of John the Baptist's followers. Afterwards, he broke away to form his own movement (John 4.3). For him baptism was a tremendous spiritual experience. It meant consciousness of the power of the Spirit in his life (Mark 1.10). It began a new life. He became conscious that he was the Son of God, that he had a special calling as the humble Servant of God (Mark 1.11).

(b) *The Twelve* Jesus called his friends to be with him and to spread his Good News about himself and the coming Kingdom he would bring (Mark 3.14). Since his message concerned people, he chose people to spread it. Hence the appointment of the 12 apostles.

(c) *Teaching* Jesus taught in synagogues (Mark 1.21) and later in the open air (Mark 4.1) about God's love and care and his requirements for people's behaviour towards God and each other. He spoke mostly about the Kingdom of God which he was inaugurating when men and women fully accept God as King of their lives.

(d) *Healing* Jesus healed people partly because he was sorry for them (Matthew 9.36) because there was little medical knowledge in those days, but also because his healings were acts of power showing that the Kingdom was at hand (Luke 11.20).

(e) *Misunderstood Messiah* Jesus was popular with the crowds so long as they thought of him as the leader who would restore sovereignty to the Jews by miracle or by force (John 6.14–15). The Twelve hardly understood him any better (Mark 8.32–3). Jesus himself came to realize that, if he were to remain faithful to his Father and his message, his mission would end in death (Mark 10.33–4).

(f) *Transfiguration* In a visionary experience, his friends learnt the truth that Jesus really was the Son of God (Mark 9.7) and was destined to die (Luke 9.31). Not long afterwards, Jesus led them towards Jerusalem, knowing that it was for the last time (Luke 18.31).

5 **Jesus's Death** Jesus knew he was to be betrayed. He waited in the Garden of Gethsemane to be 'handed over' to the Jewish authorities (Mark 14.41), who in turn 'handed him over' to the Roman secular power (Mark 15.1). Both Jews and Romans condemned him to death (see Section 8, pages 25f.)

6 **The Resurrection** Jesus's friends knew that they had seen and were in touch with Jesus within two days of his death. He was alive! This was the last thing that they were expecting, but nothing could shake their conviction. Jesus gave them their marching orders which resulted in the founding of the Church (see Section 9, pages 29f.)

7 **The Ascension** After a few weeks, they no longer saw him. But the disciples were just as convinced that they were still in touch with Jesus. He was still directing their lives but had passed to his place in Heaven (Acts 1.10–11).

8 **Whitsun** A few days later, not only the disciples but many others came to know the power of Jesus's spirit. First they were to repent (turn to God) and then to believe (accept Jesus's message) and then his Spirit was released in them (Acts 2.38) (see Section 10, pages 35f.)

5

The Meaning of Jesus

1 Jesus was fully human. He shared in ordinary family life, and grew up like us from babyhood to adulthood. He had a fully human body and human feelings. He made human friendships, and he had human limitations of knowledge.

2 Jesus prayed because he was a human being. His relationship as a human being to God was that of obedience. 'I do nothing on my own authority, but in all that I say, I have been taught by my Father' (John 8.28). 'Son though he was, he learned obedience in the school of suffering' (Hebrews 5.8).

3 Jesus was often tempted (Luke 4.13), even on one occasion sweating blood (Luke 22.44). There is nothing sinful about temptation. It is inevitable. Temptation is the inner conflict between what we want to do and what we know we ought to do.

4 From many separate biblical sources we learn that Jesus was 'without sin' (John 8.46; 2 Corinthians 5.21; Hebrews 4.15; 1 Peter 3.18). This, however, does not make him remote from us; on the contrary, 'ours is not a high priest unable to sympathize with our weaknesses, but one who, because of his likeness to us, has been tested every way, only without sin' (Hebrews 4.15).

5 Because Jesus was fully human, we find him calling himself 'Son of Man'.

6 Jesus was born into a Jewish home in the first century BC. He shared fully in this Jewish inheritance. He was born under God's providence at a time and place when the Jewish genius for religion, Greek thought and Roman justice all coincided.

7 Jesus completed God's self-disclosure to the Jewish people, and fulfilled the best hopes of their prophets. He was their 'Messiah' ('anointed' or 'chosen' one), the Christ, sent to work out God's purpose for the whole world, both Jews and Gentiles.

8 Jesus became conscious that he was in a unique relationship to God, that of a son to his father (Mark 1.11), the Son of God. His disciples learnt this at the transfiguration (Mark 9.7) and a pagan realized it at his death (Mark 15.39).

9 As Son of God, Jesus spoke with his own unique authority; not 'Thus says the Lord' but 'I say to you'. This authority is seen in his love and in his judgement, and convinces us too that he is the Son of God.

10 Jesus rose from the dead. His friends were certain that after he had died he was alive. We can know him in our lives as Son of God today (see Section 9, page 32).

11 Jesus is the full self-disclosure of God in human terms, showing us in human personality the character of God, his love and power and righteousness.

12 We would expect God to reveal himself in the highest form of life known to us – that of human beings. We would also expect him

to reveal himself in the only form of life we know from the inside – that of human beings. And so we would expect him, if he wished to reveal himself to us as fully as we can comprehend, to become man.

13 The fact that God became a human being shows us his amazing love in coming 'down to our level', to help us and to show us what he is like. God 'emptied himself' and became a very humble and self-effacing person – a servant.

NOTES

6

The Bible

1 The Bible consists of a library of books. It is in three parts: (a) the Old Testament (the Jewish Bible); (b) the Apocrypha; (c) the New Testament (about Jesus and the early Church). (The Apocrypha consists of Jewish books written in Greek and not in Hebrew which form part of the Roman Catholic Bible, but which the Church of England regards only as 'useful'.)

2 There are different kinds of writings in the Bible: folk stories (e.g. Jonah); mixtures of history and folk tales (e.g. Genesis); bare history (e.g. parts of Chronicles); hymns (e.g. Psalms); Proverbs; revelations (e.g. Daniel); Gospels, etc. In order to understand the Bible properly, it is necessary to know something about the intentions of the various writers.

3 The variety of life and literature in the Bible shows that the writers saw God in everything and everywhere.

4 The Church decided the 'canon' of Scripture (i.e. what got in and what didn't). Most books were obvious choices, but there were some borderline cases.

5 There is 'inspiration' in the Bible, but of course the writers could make errors and mistakes from time to time. This does not,

however, detract from its general trustworthiness or from its divine inspiration.

6 The Old Testament has three main uses:

   (i)   It contains some wonderful religious and moral teaching, good for its own sake.
   (ii) It shows the way in which God revealed himself progressively to his chosen people, culminating in Jesus.
   (iii) It was the Bible of Jesus and the early Church, and so we must know it to understand what they said.

The beliefs, behaviour and moral teaching in the Old Testament reflect the culture of a primitive age, and so are not to be taken as the final word for today.

7 The Old Testament sometimes contains teaching for today (e.g. 'You shall love your neighbour as yourself' (Leviticus 19.18)), but usually it cannot be applied directly to modern life. Some of its teaching has been overtaken (e.g. 'eye for eye, tooth for tooth', Deuteronomy 19.21). The food laws of the Old Covenant no longer apply (Mark 7.19), and its ritual sacrifices have been fulfilled by the sacrifice of Christ (Hebrews 7.18–19).

8 The Gospels give us four portraits of Jesus, each with its author's distinctive style, but essentially in agreement. These are the only reliable sources for the life and teaching of Jesus. (There are other so-called Gospels, known as 'apocryphal', late in origin, which may contain a few fragments of Jesus's teaching.) Although the Gospels are not intended to be biographies in the modern sense, they convey the essence of his life and teaching, and are an inspiration to read. The Gospels were not written until the original eyewitnesses were dying out.

9 St Mark's Gospel was the earliest to be written, and shows simplicity, realism and reserve, especially about Jesus's Messiahship. St Matthew's Gospel shows apocalyptic and ecclesiastical interests, and concentrates on Jesus's teaching as the consummation of Old Testament religion.

10 Just as St Luke's Gospel shows how the Good News of Jesus came from Nazareth to Jerusalem, Luke's Acts show how it was taken from Jerusalem to Rome. Without this history of the early Church we should not be able to make sense of the rest of the New Testament.

11 The Epistles contain the earliest writings of the New Testament. They consist of letters of St Paul, etc., and give a 'normative' account of the Christian religion (belief, worship, practice) from its beginning. The Book of Revelation is an imaginative work of prophecy, full of images taken from the Old Testament.

12 The New Testament is not infallible, but it is the Church's guide and 'norm'. Of course it needs reinterpretation in every age, and especially today. Many modern issues (e.g. abortion, nuclear deterrence) had not arisen in biblical days, while other teaching (e.g. on the subjection of women) reflects the culture of a past age. While there is a valid religious point underlying biblical teaching, these truths would often be expressed today in different teaching.

13 The Church of England contains people with differing views about the use of Scripture, but it has long been a key principle that 'whatsoever is not read therein, nor may be proved thereby, is not to be required of any man, that it should be believed as an article of the Faith or be thought requisite or necessary for salvation' (Article VI of the Church of England's Thirty-nine Articles).

7

Sin and Forgiveness

1 If we grow up in an atmosphere where God's love is known and experienced, we feel safe and secure and want to share his love with others. If we also grow up in a family where we know 'how far we can go' in the ways in which we are allowed to behave, this helps us to feel more safe and secure.

2 If we have not experienced God's love as children or if we have not experienced its reflection in the security of our parents' love for us and in the security that their discipline gives us, we become insecure inside ourselves. This leads to estrangement from God.

3 Lacking the security and happiness of knowing ourselves to be the beloved children of God, we try to bolster ourselves up by snatching from or jeering at others, or gratifying ourselves, as second-best substitutes for True Living.

4 *Sin* is basically estrangement from God. It is not a matter of feelings, like guilt, but a matter of a wrong relationship. This estrangement shows itself in wrong ('sinful') attitudes of mind; and these may result in wrong acts ('actual sins'). It is easy if we are estranged from God to think that we have good motives, but unknown to ourselves we may be doing things which displease

God (e.g. those Pharisees who thought they were pleasing God by fasting but were really trying to earn merit for themselves and to prove to themselves and to others how good they were).

5 Before we were old enough to know the difference between right and wrong ('moral consciousness'), we could not be held responsible for sin. But when we can choose, then we begin to be responsible for our moral choices. Moral responsibility is part of what it means to be created 'in the image of God'.

6 It is not possible for us to apportion blame for our own or anyone's sins. They are partly our own fault, partly the result of our parents' upbringing, partly due to our own surroundings. Our personal share of the blame is known not to us, but to God alone. However, unless we are very sick indeed, we have some real freedom of choice, and so we have some real responsibility for our sins.

7 We are all creatures of habit. Just as doing good may become habitual, so also can sins. **Habitual sins** are often not quickly or easily left behind.

8 **Guilt** is different from sin. It is a very unpleasant *feeling* inside ourselves, telling us that we have done wrong. It can be useful (just as it is useful to feel pain if we hurt ourselves). But guilt is easily attached to attitudes and actions which are quite free from sin, and it is possible also to act sinfully without feeling guilt. Inappropriate guilt feelings need psychotherapy rather than forgiveness. The best way to test ourselves is not by guilt feelings but by the two Great Commandments (to love God and our neighbour as ourselves).

9 How did sin arise?

    (a) The Garden of Eden is a 'myth', i.e. a historical tale embodying spiritual truth. Even though it is not historically accurate, the 'myth' contains great truths (e.g. trying to pass the blame to others, wanting to do just what we are told not to do). It shows the universality of sin and sets it within human history.

    (b) Human beings are the result of evolution, and shaped by natural selection. Self-centredness and aggression were essential at every stage of evolution.

    (c) Human beings naturally inherit this self-centredness ('original sin') and without it babies could not survive.

10 Actual sins may be trivial, or very serious. They show us 'missing the mark' (the meaning of one of the New Testament words for sin). As the Lord's Prayer makes clear, in order for sins to be forgiven, we need:

    (i) acknowledgement of them together with repentance ('Forgive us our sins');

    (ii) a forgiving spirit towards others ('as we forgive those who sin against us').

11 Fortunately, even though we so often commit sins, we are also capable of great goodness: we never lose 'the image of God'. No one is so bad that the case is hopeless: there is always the offer of a fresh start.

12 Far more serious than actual sins is the state of estrangement from God, what is sometimes called just 'sin'. This needs special action from God. We find this in the cross.

8

The Death of Jesus

1 Jesus 'handed himself over' and put himself in the power of his enemies. His death shows us God allowing humans to do the worst they can to him. It shows God caring for us as much as that. It shows God forgiving and accepting us, not as we should be, but as we are, as bad as we can be, with no reservations on his part at all.

2 Jesus's crucifixion was ordered by Pontius Pilate, the Roman Governor, probably in AD 33 after a trial in the Jewish High Court. The Jews today are in no way responsible for his death.

3 Jesus died by being nailed to a wooden stake, with his hands nailed to a cross bar. It was the normal way of execution by Romans for criminals. Death was the result of shock, weakness and asphyxiation.

4 Jesus's death shows up very ordinary human weaknesses:

    (a) One of his own friends betrayed him.
    (b) The rest let him down by fleeing in fear.
    (c) The Roman Governor knew he was innocent, but condemned him because he was frightened that otherwise he would be sacked.
    (d) The High Priest thought that it was worth a man's death to keep in with the ruling power.

(e)   The Pharisees thought that Jesus was religiously dangerous because he upset their religious convictions.

(f)   The Sadducees feared that, if he lived, they would lose their religious status.

(g)   Herod laughed at him.

(h)   The Zealots had no use for him because he would not use force.

(i)   The crowds were led by their cheerleaders.

5 Jesus suffered terribly on the cross in various ways:

(a)   He suffered physical agony – 'a most cruel death', a Roman historian called it.

(b)   He suffered spiritually – like us, he did not want to die.

(c)   He suffered the taunts of others, mockery, betrayal, indifference and weakness.

(d)   He suffered the loss of his Father's presence – nothing was left. He was stripped bare. He hung in the void. 'My God, my God, why hast thou forsaken me?'

6 *What the Cross Means*

(a)   *Sacrifice* is used of Jesus's death to show that it was costly and involved death.

(b)   *Reconciliation* is used to show that man is no longer estranged from God.

(c)   *Justification* is used to show that we have all been 'put in the right' with God (i.e. accepted).

(d)   *Ransom* is used to show that his death was costly and that it brings liberation.

(e)   *Triumph* is used because by his death Jesus passed beyond the powers of evil, and so triumphed over them.

7 *What the Cross Is Not*

(a) The angry Father appeasing his wrath by taking it out on his loving Son. Such a viewpoint betrays a sub-Christian idea of God. God may be angry at sins, but he always loves the sinner. His feelings are not swayed by the punishment of anyone.

(b) The Son standing in my place to take the punishment that I ought to have. Such a view is immoral. In any case no one person could suffer the whole world's punishments. And even if he could, this would mean that everyone could go on sinning without any fear of punishment.

8 *What the Cross Is*

(a) God does for us what we cannot do for ourselves.
God in action shows his love for everyone by the death of his Son on behalf of us (not 'instead of us') as our representative. By so doing he takes away our guilt.

(b) God, by accepting on the cross the worst that human beings can do to him, draws the sting of our resentments against him, and removes our basic fears and insecurities.

(c) Jesus's sense of abandonment by God on the cross ('My God, my God, why have you forsaken me?') finds an echo in those times when we also feel abandoned in adversity. In union with him, we too can still cling to God and share in the joy of Jesus's subsequent resurrection.

9 We have been accepted. We can accept ourselves. We can begin to return God's love to him, and to hand it on to our neighbours. We are no longer estranged from God, but reconciled to him and to our fellows.

10 The basic Christian symbol is not the crucifix but the *empty* cross because Jesus triumphed over death by his resurrection. The resurrection does not add to the victory of the cross, but it does publicly placard it for all who are willing to see.

NOTES

9

The Resurrection

1 Jesus would have been utterly unknown today (except perhaps for an obscure reference in some Jewish document) if his earliest followers had not been utterly convinced that, against all expectation, he had been raised from the dead. Since the fact of the resurrection is central to the Christian story, and the meaning of the resurrection is central to the Christian gospel, it is worth while looking at the evidence in greater detail.

2 Jesus three times foretold his coming death and resurrection in the Gospels, but the disciples did not seem to grasp the meaning of what he said until after his resurrection. At Jesus's arrest the Twelve all forsook him and fled (Mark 14.30). Although Peter subsequently followed him when Jesus was taken away for questioning (Mark 14.54), and John (if he was the beloved disciple) is said to have stood with Mary at the foot of the cross (John 19.26), none of the Twelve were expecting anything but the collapse of his mission, and found it hard to believe that he had been raised from the dead (Luke 24.11).

3 There is no account of the actual resurrection itself in the four Gospels. The early Church was convinced that he had been raised for three reasons:

(i) The tomb was empty.
(ii) Jesus appeared to them after his death.
(iii) They felt his presence among them.

4 *The Empty Tomb*

According to the Gospels, the tomb was found empty by women coming to complete the burial rites which had been interrupted by the onset of the Jewish sabbath. Various explanations of this have been given:

(a) *Jesus had not died* Yet St John's Gospel makes it clear that he was dead (John 19.32ff.) and in any case the subsequent appearances are not compatible with One who had just recovered from a moribund condition.

(b) *The women in the dark went to the wrong tomb* It is not really possible that belief in his resurrection rested on a mistake!

(c) *Jesus's body was never placed in Joseph's tomb* Executed Jews were buried usually in a common grave. But there is good reason to accept the detailed story in which Joseph of Arimathea sought special permission from the Governor that the body be laid in his tomb adjacent to the scene of the crucifixion.

(d) *Jesus's body was removed from the tomb* It was forbidden by Jewish law to touch a dead body, and it is hard to see any motivation for the Jews to remove the body. According to Matthew 28.11ff., the Jews accused the disciples of stealing the body, but no adequate explanation can be given for their motive in so doing. It is inconceivable that they deliberately stole the body in order to pretend that he had risen from the dead, for the narratives show that they were convinced that he had been raised.

(e) *The story of the empty tomb is a later invention* Yet the tradition of the empty tomb in all four Gospels is clear and unequivocal, and takes us back to a shortish period after Jesus's death. It can be traced back further to within two or three years of his death in the writings of St Paul (1 Corinthians 15; Galatians 1.16).

(f) *God raised Jesus from the dead*   This has always been an integral part of the Gospel, and the evidence favours it as the true explanation.

5 *The Resurrection Appearances*

Jesus appeared to his disciples after his death, and not to his enemies (except, later, to St Paul as an 'abnormal birth' (1 Corinthians 15.8)). Appearances are found in three Gospels, in Acts and in 1 Corinthians 15.5ff. According to St Matthew's Gospel, Jesus appeared in Galilee; to St Luke's, in Jerusalem; to St John's, in both. St Mark's Gospel ends abruptly before an appearance is described. The pattern of most stories is a short description of the situation, then Jesus's appearance, followed by a greeting, a recognition, culminating with a word of command by Jesus.

6 Jesus is not always immediately recognized in these appearances. He can pass through doors, can materialize anywhere, can eat and drink, and is susceptible of being touched. He can suddenly dematerialize. These resurrection appearances are not unlike paranormal experiences sometimes called 'veridical hallucinations' which can take place shortly after the death of a loved one. But the stories differ in that Jesus usually has an authoritative word of command for his followers, the appearances continue for longer, and up to 500 people saw him at once (1 Corinthians 15.6).

7 *Christian Experience*

The early Christians were convinced of the presence of the risen Lord among them and in them, as indeed Christians have been so convinced in their own experience down the centuries.
On the evidence of the empty tomb, the resurrection appearances and Christian experience, Christians believe even against modern so-called 'scientific' scepticism that the evidence favours belief in the resurrection of Jesus.

8 *The Ascension*

According to the Lucan writings (Gospel and Acts) after a period of 40 days Jesus appeared to his disciples no more, but was seen to ascend into heaven, and (apart from occasional visions such as that given to St Stephen) he communicated thenceforward to his disciples through his Spirit. These stories of his ascension are told in such a way as to show Jesus fulfilling (in St Luke's Gospel) the role of Tobit (Tobit 12.20–21) and (in the Acts) that of Elijah (1 Kings 19). In St John's Gospel the ascension is seen in very close connection with the resurrection (John 21.17). In St Paul's writings there is no distinction made between the resurrection and the ascension. It seems most probable that the appearances of the risen Lord did cease after a time, but there was not a particular act of ascension.

9 *The Meaning of Jesus's Resurrection in the Gospels*

(a) *St Mark's Gospel* sees Jerusalem as a dark tunnel through which Jesus must go to his vindication at his resurrection appearance in Galilee which is invested with the awe, mystery and fearfulness of the final event.

(b) *St Matthew's Gospel* sees the resurrection as a foretaste of the final event, presaged by an appearance on the mountain in Galilee in which Jesus is invested with power and authority.

But before the final event itself, there must be a mission of
teaching and preaching to all nations.

(c) *St Luke's Gospel* sees the resurrection as the completion of
one great phase in God's plan for his world. First there is the
period of Israel (the Law and the Prophets); then the period
of Jesus, which gives a foretaste of future salvation; and
finally the time between the coming of Jesus and the final
act, the period of the Church and of the Spirit. (This is the
last age, but Luke does not tell us it will be short.) In this
scheme, Jerusalem is the place where the good news is
preached, and where the ascension takes place.

(d) *St John's Gospel*, like St Luke's, sees the resurrection as rooted
in history, but the author is also insistent on turning the
mind of his readers to the invisible realities which give these
events their meaning. St John regards the resurrection both
as pointing to a final event (with an appearance in Galilee)
and also as the occasion when the Spirit is poured out (as
the Jerusalem appearance makes clear, John 20.22).

Each of the four Gospels has its different details and its particular
nuance about the meaning of the resurrection, but there is un-
animous affirmation of the fact of the resurrection, and its
central importance for the vindication of Jesus's ministry.

10 *The Meaning of the Resurrection for St Paul*

(i) God affirms Jesus by raising him from the dead and attests
his lowly ministry of service and suffering (Romans 1.4), and
his true divine status is made clear by stories of his ascension
(Ephesians 1.20).

(ii) The resurrection of Jesus is 'the Father's Amen to the Son's
"It is finished"' (Philippians 2.9ff.). It is the public proclama-
tion of the meaning of the cross.

(iii) The resurrection shows Jesus as 'the first fruits of the harvest

of the dead' (1 Corinthians 15.20), i.e. the One who antici-
pates the final destiny of all, and who inaugurates a new era
of God's power in the world.

(iv) The resurrection shows the triumph of good over evil, and
the conquest of sin and death by the power of God (Romans
6.8; 8.1).

(v) The resurrection is shared by Christians through union with
Christ, so that his risen life works in and through Christians.

11 *The Meaning of the Resurrection for Us Today*

The chief meaning of the resurrection is that the claims of the
Christian gospel are true. The risen Jesus in his spiritual presence
is always with us, wherever we are, especially in worship. He
himself said: 'Where two or three are gathered together in my
name, there am I in the midst of them' (Matthew 18.20).

NOTES

10

The Holy Spirit

1   The Holy Spirit is God in action in our world. In the poetic description of creation in Genesis, we read that the earth was without form and void, with darkness over the face of the abyss and 'the Spirit hovering over the surface of the waters' (Genesis 1.2). Today we might say that from the moment of the Big Bang onwards the Holy Spirit has been at work in the shaping and development of the universe.

2   The Holy Spirit is at work in human beings. The Greek word for Spirit is the same as that for breath or wind, and the work of the Spirit is invisible, powerful and life-giving. In the creeds he is described as 'the Lord, Giver of Life'. 'The Lord God formed a man from the dust of the ground and breathed into his nostrils the breath (spirit) of life. Thus the man became a living creature' (Genesis 2.7).

3   God puts his Spirit in men and women (Isaiah 42.1). He brings righteousness. He also gives understanding (Isaiah 11.2) and wisdom (Exodus 28.3) and strength and power (Micah 3.8). The Spirit inspires human beings with all that is good and true and life-enhancing. He is at work in all the great world faiths where there is an authentic experience of God and a true enhancement of life.

The Spirit in the Life of Jesus

4   The Spirit is given to the prophets of Israel. Through the Spirit
Mary conceived, and Jesus was born. At his baptism in the
Jordan, Jesus had a special experience of the Spirit through which
he knew that he was God's Son, and called to be his servant. The
Spirit drove Jesus to temptation, and in the Spirit Jesus did
mighty works of healing and preached the good news of God's
Kingdom. At his death he 'handed over the Spirit' ('gave up the
ghost').

5   The Spirit that was in Jesus during his lifetime was poured out
from Jesus on to his Church at its foundation on the first Whit
Sunday.

The Spirit in Us

6   As members of the Church the Spirit is at work in all that makes
us more alive, more human, more like our Lord Jesus Christ.
'That which is born of the flesh is flesh, and that which is born of
the Spirit is Spirit.' The flesh stands for what is outward, material,
superficial. The Spirit is the Divine working in us, making us
authentic, true and God-centred. To be born again is to put aside
superficial living and to be open to the Spirit of God.

7   At baptism we are introduced into the Spirit-filled sphere of the
Church. We share in the Holy Spirit, and so we are united with
our fellow members in Christ. The Spirit gives us feelings of joy
and peace and assurance: he also gives us wisdom and insight.

8   Individuals may be given particular gifts of the Spirit, which can
range from administration to speaking in tongues. The Renewal
Movement today has brought many to a new awareness of the
Spirit within them, and to a fresh understanding of prayer and

charismatic gifts, which may include healing or prophecy. These gifts, however, should always be for the building up of the Church and never divisive. They should always be subordinate to the greatest gift of all, Christian love.

The Spirit and the Holy Trinity

9 The Spirit proceeds from the mysterious being of God himself, one of the three ways in which God makes himself known as Father, Son or Holy Spirit.

NOTES

11

Prayer (1)

Why Do We Pray?

1 Prayer is the way in which we consciously realize our relationship with God. It is the opening of the heart and the mind to him. There are as many ways of praying as there are ways of relating ourselves to him.

2 Not to pray is to deny our Christian faith. In prayer we find within ourselves new and hidden depths of being – a practical expression of our faith in the Holy Spirit at work in us. In prayer we find that Jesus brings us straight into the presence of God: in prayer we put into practice our conviction that through Christ we have access to the Father. In prayer we lose ourselves in the mystery and majesty of God: in terms of the Christian faith, through Christ in the Spirit we come to the Father.

How Do We Pray?

3 Silence is the beginning of prayer – not just outward silence, but the stilling of our inner turmoil, the quietening of our wandering thoughts and unruly desires. It is more important that God should be able to speak to us than that we should speak to him. We need to learn to pray, just as once we had to learn to talk and to listen. When we are attentive to God and open to his grace,

when we cease to worry about ourselves, then we are praying. Words don't matter.

4   Most people need some aids to enable them to come into God's presence. A book of prayers, a sentence or two from the Bible, a book of spirituality or devotion; these can help to ease us into God's presence and to be silent with him. Don't expect God to send you a personal message through this kind of prayer. Simply be grateful that you have been with God, and have been refreshed by his grace.

Praying with the Imagination

5   Some people find that they can pray with their imagination, so long as they keep it under control. For this you need to be able to see pictures in your mind's eye. Choose some scene from the Gospels in which Jesus figures. Imagine you are there yourself, ask yourself what Jesus is saying to you within that scene, and then translate it into your ordinary everyday life.

Praying with the Bible

6   If you don't have a pictorial imagination – and if you do! – choose some passage for Bible study. Use the Bible sensibly. Don't just open it at random, but treat it with intelligent devotion. You need a modern translation and some Bible notes to help you understand what the Bible authors meant – ask your vicar, there are plenty of these notes around. Take a passage – not too long – find out what it means, ponder it word for word; ask yourself what (if anything) it means for you today, and whether, as a result, you ought to change anything in your life.

Must I Kneel?

7   You don't have to kneel down to pray. Choose whatever posture of the body suits you best. We all need a regular time of day and a minimum time of prayer each day. Perhaps five minutes morning and evening? Don't set your sights too high, or you will get discouraged at your own performance!

Feelings of Success and Failure

8   There are times when God seems very close in prayer, and he fills you with feelings of joy and assurance, and helps you to pray in ways you did not dream of. There are times too when God seems infinitely far off and remote, and we are aware not of the Real Presence but a Real Absence. We are sent 'growing pains' to make us mature in our spiritual life. We have to learn to rely less on our feelings about God, and to put more and more trust in God himself. In our prayers there are times when we feel that we are risen with Christ; but there are times too when we know we are crucified with him.

9   Many people are spiritually hungry and want to learn to pray but are reluctant to ask someone's help. Find out from your church if there is a 'retreat' or 'quiet day' or 'quiet afternoon': don't be frightened of getting help from the clergy. If you feel your prayers are too chaotic to reveal to another person, remember God sees the desires of the heart and the intentions of the soul, and wants to help.

NOTES

12

Prayer (2)

1 Worship means giving God the worth that is due to him alone. We open our hearts to his glory, we are awed by his infinite wisdom and power in bringing the universe into being, we remind ourselves of his love for us in sending us his Son, we feel humbled by his mercy and compassion and his ever-present grace. It may be helpful to use the words of the 'Holy, Holy, Holy' (from the Holy Communion) or some songs from the Book of Revelation, to give verbal expression to our acts of adoration.

2 *Thanking God*

We take so much in life for granted. We are more likely to ask God for what we haven't got than to thank him for what we have. It is instructive to go through the ordinary events of a day, and see how much of it is really an occasion for which we should give thanks to God: food, friends, health, security. Many lives are twisted because they are starved of thanksgiving. Gratitude is the mark of a true Christian. A deeply committed person can even thank God for what he has been denied as well as what he has been given, for the marks of the cross as well as for the signs of God's presence. (If you find thanksgiving difficult, go through the General Thanksgiving clause by clause.)

CONFIRMATION NOTEBOOK

3 *Saying Sorry*

God loves to forgive. But we cannot take this for granted. We need to know how much and how deeply we have fallen short. A very good way of self-examination is to measure our lives by the Beatitudes (Matthew 5.3–10). We can do wrong through negligence, weakness, or through our own deliberate fault. Jesus, in the Lord's Prayer, placed only one condition on our receiving God's forgiveness – that we should show a truly forgiving spirit to others. When in our private prayers we make our confession to God, we should always end by thanking God for his forgiveness and for his grace which enables us to make a fresh start.

4 *Praying for Others*

When we pray for others and for ourselves, we need not be worried that God knows our needs before we begin. Of course he does. Prayer is our sharing with him our concerns and our wants about others and about ourselves. We tell him about the deepest desires of our hearts, confident that we are speaking in the presence of our loving Father. God is not likely to respond to our prayers if we use them as a substitute for our own action! Prayer and life should be all of a piece. Naturally we must not pray for any action that would be unworthy of God, or for anything that is unworthy of ourselves, but everything in our hearts of which we are not ashamed we can place before our loving Father.

5 *The Effect of Prayer*

When we pray for others and for ourselves, we can do so with confidence, in the faith that our prayers will always be answered. God as it were releases his power in the world through the prayers of men and women. But we must not suppose that God will always answer our prayers in the way that we want. We must be open to whatever answer he sends.

42

6 *Planning Prayers*

We need a routine of prayer, but if we are to avoid getting stale, we need variety in the ways we pray, and even in the times we pray. All relationships need to be kept fresh, including our relationship with God. We don't have to keep our prayers for set times of prayer. We can shoot 'arrow prayers' to God at any time during the day – 'Thank you, God, for that', 'O God, please give your help to that crippled old lady.' Learn to pray over the daily paper or the radio and TV news – 'Help that person, please Lord', 'Give a spirit of peace in that industrial dispute.' But we must not let prayer prevent us from concentrating on our job. When driving a car, it is more important to drive safely than to pray for people in the car approaching you!

NOTES

13

The Sacraments

Nature and Human Nature

1 God addresses us in a way suited to our nature; not merely in words, but also through the material world. The beauty of nature is an expression of God's majesty just as much as the words of Scripture.

2 Human beings need more than words in their personal relationships with one another. A handshake can mean so much more than a mere word of welcome, a kiss more than a spoken endearment. We are our bodies as much as we are our feelings and our minds. We need body language as much as spoken language to converse.

3 Many symbolic actions or ceremonies can speak to us with a special meaning (e.g. kneeling down to pray, as a sign of our dependence on God), but God sets apart some for special use in his Church. If God sets apart some of the natural world in this special way, this means that all nature is good: it can all be the medium of his presence and his activity.

The Sacraments

4 God has set apart certain symbolic actions which we call sacraments. He takes ordinary human activities, such as washing and

eating, and gives them a special meaning (spiritual washing, spiritual food, etc.).

5   There are seven sacraments so called, either specially ordered by Jesus or derived from the New Testament:

(a) Baptism
(b) Holy Communion   } 'Sacraments of the Gospel'
(c) Confirmation
(d) Absolution
(e) Marriage
(f) Ordination
(g) Unction (for the sick)

More than Symbols

6   Human beings are very dependent on their feelings so far as the practice of their religion is concerned. Sacraments are particularly suited to the human condition because they deliver people from enslavement to feelings. Sacraments are given by God, and provided that they are received in faith, we are promised the grace of God, whatever we may or may not feel. While sacraments need to be subjectively received in faith, their objectivity meets our need for assurance.

Abuse of Sacraments

7   If sacraments are not received in faith, they tend to degenerate into magic, so that the words and actions seem to be a kind of formula guaranteeing and even compelling the special action of God. It is this abuse of sacraments in the past which has caused suspicion of them in some circles.

Why Sacraments Help

8   Because sacraments are symbolic actions, God can communicate to us through them without our having to articulate precisely what is being done. And so sacraments are particularly helpful to those who find it hard to verbalize their faith. At the same time, words do illuminate the action of a sacrament, and also the reverse. Hence the conjunction of word and sacrament. The word is addressed to the discursive mind, and the sacrament speaks to those deeper levels of consciousness where imagination and the subconscious are moved by sign and symbol.

9   All Christian sacraments come to us from Jesus Christ through his Church. The Church is sacramental, inasmuch as it is an outward sign (the congregation of Christian people) of an inward and spiritual grace (the Body of Christ, or People of God). Jesus Christ is himself the supreme sacrament, in whom the Word (inward and spiritual grace) was made flesh (the outward sign). All sacraments have these two aspects (e.g. bread and wine in the Eucharist as signs of the Body and Blood of Christ).

NOTES

14

The Meaning of Holy Communion

1 Obedience

In the earliest account of the Last Supper, Jesus says to the Twelve in instituting the Holy Communion, 'Do this as a memorial of me' (1 Corinthians 11.24). He ordered the Twelve to continue this eucharistic action ('Do this', not 'Say this'); and when the Holy Communion is celebrated, it is not an optional extra, but a necessary part of Christian obedience. This is what the word 'Liturgy' means, by which the service is sometimes known.

2 Memorial

When Jesus said, 'Do this as a memorial of me', he was using a word which signified much more than a subjective act of recollection. 'Memorial' here means rather a making real of the past in the present, in the same way as we may enjoy a foretaste of the future. We look back to the Last Supper as well as forward to the Messianic Banquet in the Kingdom of God, as we are fed here and now with the sacramental reality of the Body and Blood of Christ.

3 Eucharist

In the biblical accounts of the Last Supper, Jesus gave thanks over the bread and wine. The word 'Eucharist' means thanksgiving.

Christians give thanks not only for the world of nature, but also for the whole drama of Christian salvation; for the coming of Christ, for his death, resurrection and ascension, for the gift of the Holy Spirit, and for the promise of final fulfilment.

4 Sharing

At the Last Supper, Jesus did not himself share in the bread and wine, but the Twelve shared it among themselves. In the Holy Communion, the People of God share together in the whole eucharistic action, and the priest acts as the President of the assembly. The action includes offering ('He took'), sharing ('He broke'), consecration ('He blessed'), and receiving ('He gave'). The service is not a matter of private piety but of public worship.

5 The Mass

The word 'Mass' is derived from the closing words of the old Roman rite ('*Ite, missa est*' – 'Go, you are sent out into the world'). The Eucharist enacts sacramentally the same pattern in our lives as when we live them in the world. With our relationship to God renewed in Christ through the Eucharist, we are sent out into the world to offer our lives to God, to share them with others, to be consecrated in Christ and to find Christ in our neighbours, especially in the outcast and deprived.

6 The Holy Communion

The service is not a sacred ritual which is remote from the rest of life. 'The consecration of a part marks the destiny of the whole' (B. F. Westcott). We meet Christ through the bread and wine of the Eucharist, so that he may be the unseen host at all our meals. We are united with Christ sacramentally in the Eucharist so that all our ordinary life may be lived in communion with him.

7   *The Universal Church*

All the historic churches of Christendom preserve the same structure of the Eucharist, which has been handed down the centuries from the primitive Church. In this structure the Ministry of the Word always precedes the Ministry of the Sacrament. In some churches 'vestments' (the 'dress clothes' of the first century) are worn as a symbol of continuity. Some celebrations may be simple and bare, while others may be marked by considerable ceremonial, so that the outward senses as well as the heart are involved in worship. However it is celebrated, the meaning is always the same.

NOTES

15

Holy Communion
(*Common Worship*)

1   The services of all churches follow a similar structure of Holy
    Communion as explained below.

    The Church of England authorized for use from 2002, in addition
    to the Holy Communion Service in the Book of Common Prayer,
    new services in *Common Worship*. There are two forms of service,
    each in contemporary and in conventional language. Order 2 is
    more like the Book of Common Prayer; Order 1, which is
    described below, has developed from the Alternative Service
    Book, which has now been superseded by *Common Worship*.

2   The essential and invariable parts of the Service reveal its twofold
    basic structure. First, the Ministry of the Word, in which the
    people and the priest:

    (a)   greet each other in the Lord's name;
    (b)   confess their sins and are assured of God's forgiveness
          (invitation, confession and absolution);
    (c)   keep silence and pray a Collect (the prayer for the week);
    (d)   proclaim and respond to the Word of God (through scripture
          readings, sermon and creed);
    (e)   Pray for the Church and for the world (intercessory prayers).

3   The second part of the Service is the Ministry of the Sacrament. The priest and people:

(a)   may exchange the Peace (a symbol of fellowship);
(b)   prepare the table (laid with bread and wine which the President takes in his or her hands);
(c)   pray the Eucharistic Prayer (using one of eight options);
(d)   break the bread (as Jesus did at the Last Supper);
(e)   receive communion (the consecrated bread and wine);
(f)   depart with God's blessing.

4   There is a considerable variety of additional material which may or may not be used, and which is not very suitable for discussion here. The Service in *Common Worship* repays study, in order to grasp its richness and flexibility.

NOTES

16

Holiness

1 Holiness is the goal of every true Christian. 'Holy' means 'set apart for God'. A holy person is not gloomy and unnatural, but 'whole' and therefore happy. That is why holiness, whenever we see it in others, is always attractive.

2 Holiness has nothing to do with book-learning. It concerns your heart and will, the real you. Jesus said: 'Where your treasure is, there will your heart be also.'

3 *How on earth could someone like me ever be holy?*
In active terms holiness means doing God's will, in passive terms accepting whatever the present moment brings.

4 *How can I know the will of God?*

  (i) By my own *talents*. God usually wants people to do a job which suits them.
  (ii) By *opportunity;* but I may have to create the opportunity.
  (iii) By *inclination*. God doesn't always ask me to crucify myself. I work better if I like it.
  (iv) Sometimes God calls me to great sacrifice, sometimes God shows his will by 'slow pressure', sometimes by overpowering conviction. My *feelings* need to be tested.

5 *How can I accept the present moment?*

   (i) Self-discipline can make me comply outwardly.

 (ii) Inner acceptance can't be forced. It just happens.

(iii) This inner acceptance takes a very long time.

(iv) It comes when I no longer want to bother about myself or others, but trust fully in God.

6 *Discipleship*

Christian discipleship means a succession of fresh starts, always from a fresh starting-point. Don't expect quick results or an even progress.

7 Discipleship is not easy (nothing worth while is). Sometimes you will feel marvellous; sometimes you will be lost in 'the dark night of the soul'.

8 Everyone has a different journey. The saints have gone ahead. They are an inspiration and a guide. Find out which one can help you.

9 Jesus said: 'Be perfect, as your Heavenly Father is perfect.' He didn't mean that each person must reach the same excellence but that each can fully respond in his or her own way to God.

10 Each person has his or her own way of holiness. But a Christian will always follow Christ, or some particular facet of Christ's life.

11 *The saints*

Saints are those of proven holiness. There are thousands in the Christian Church recognized as saints, including the apostles, martyrs (those killed because of Christ), missionaries, mystics, teachers of the faith, social reformers, bishops, monks and nuns and lay people of a holy life. Saints are commemorated on the day of their death. *Common Worship* has in its calendar 25 'red letter' saints (important saints), 103 saints and 125 commemorations of holy people.

12 *Why the saints are important*

The saints are important because they are examples to us of a holy life, and often a person finds a particular saint as a model for herself or himself. We can ask saints to pray for us. This is not praying to the saints, but asking them for their prayers to God. In the creed we say we believe in the 'communion of saints', meaning that we are linked with them in fellowship although they are divided from us by death.

13 The Bible is not the only book about God. Many of the following 'classics' on holiness are in paperback:

Anon
> *The Cloud of Unknowing*

Augustine, St
> *Confessions*

Baxter, Richard
> *The Saints' Everlasting Rest*

Bonhoeffer, Dietrich
> *The Cost of Discipleship*

Bunyan, John
> *Pilgrim's Progress*

Caussade, J. P. de
> *Abandonment to Divine Providence*

Francis of Assisi, St
The Little Flowers

Francis of Sales, St
Introduction to the Devout Life

Hügel, Baron Friedrich von
Letters to a Niece

Mother Julian of Norwich
Revelations of Divine Love

Kierkegaard, Søren
Journals

Lewis, C. S.
Letters to Andrew

Pascal, Blaise
Penséces

Thomas à Kempis
The Imitation of Christ

Vanstone, W. H.
The Stature of Waiting

Williams, H. A.
The True Wilderness

NOTES

17

Heaven and Hell

What happens when I die?

1 No one knows exactly what will happen to a person after death. All blueprints are guesswork.

Why believe in life after death?

2 No one knows how personality can survive death. Our character seems bound up with our glands, brain, etc. Yet there is evidence of survival. God's work in us is so obviously incomplete. He would not create people who are not mature enough to complete his plan for them, so there must be a future life for them to attain full maturity. It is the witness of Christians that 'Jesus lives'. The Christian doctrine of 'resurrection' points to the continuance of the whole personality, not just a part of it.

3 Even in this life we catch a glimpse of God's love and we can exult in life; but our faith in life after death is grounded in (a) God's love for us, and (b) our acknowledgement of our incomplete development. God has more in store for us.

4 We are not just individuals. Personality needs relationship to exist. Therefore what happens after death is not just a question for individuals, but for people as a whole.

What is heaven?

5 The final destiny of human existence is to share the life of God. This involves ability to respond to his love.

6 In this world we are so to develop and deepen our characters that we may be more self-aware and responsive and sensitive to God.

7 Since we are people of this world, the Christian is very concerned with material circumstances as the soil out of which the flower of human character must grow.

8 Heaven describes the state of eternal and full response to God's love; hell describes a state of eternal inability to respond to love.

What is judgement?

9 Pictures of the Last Judgement given in the New Testament should not obscure the fact, also given in the New Testament, that we pass judgement on ourselves.

10 Thus heaven is not a reward to the good, or hell a punishment for the bad. God always acts lovingly and gives us that state of being for which our character has fitted us.

Is there a second chance?

11 Moral choices confront us as though they were ultimate choices pointing to heaven or hell. But since 'God will have all to be saved' (1 Timothy 2.4) it seems improbable that anyone's sole chance of development lies in this life. Yet this life is the only one we know.

12 Purgatory stands for the truths (a) that on our deathbed we are not yet ready to be fully responsive to God's love, (b) that self-

awareness is often painful, and (c) that God continues to love us and to lead us towards himself after death.

13 We cannot know the details of our future or final destiny. But we do know it cannot be dull to be closer to the Fount of all Being, the Source of all Love, and the Creator of all Things.

NOTES

18

Christian Festivals and Fasts

Festivals

1   The most important festival of the Christian Year is Easter Day, when we commemorate the Resurrection of Jesus and his spiritual presence in us and among us.

2   Christmas is the most popular festival today, because it marks the birth of baby Jesus and the beginning of the Christian family.

3   Other principal festivals are Festivals of Our Lord:

> The Epiphany (the Magi's gifts to Jesus) on 6 January.
> The Presentation of Christ in the Temple (Candlemas).
> Maundy Thursday (three days before Easter; the institution of the Eucharist).
> Ascension Day (40 days after Easter; marks the Ascension of Jesus).

4   Other principal festivals are:

> Pentecost (50 days after Easter; the giving of the Holy Spirit).
> All Saints' Day (2 November).
> The Festivals of Apostles, including the Conversion of St Paul.

Fasts

5   According to the Book of Common Prayer, Days of Fasting or Abstinence include every Friday (as a commemoration of Christ's death) and the 40 days of Lent (the period before Easter); but the new *Common Worship* omits this.

6   Nonetheless there is a common custom of giving up something during Lent, since abstinence is a mark of self-discipline and can deepen spirituality. Lent begins with Ash Wednesday, so called because of the custom of marking the forehead with ash. Good Friday (the day of Jesus's crucifixion) is now a working day, but it should be specially marked by some form of abstinence and (if possible) by worship.

Three marks of the Christian life

7   Almsgiving, fasting and prayer are by tradition three marks of the Christian life, and these are emphasized by Jesus in the 'Sermon on the Mount' (Matthew 6.1–18).

NOTES

19

Other Religions

1 Britain has now become a multi-faith society. Although this has
been for many centuries a Christian land, and in some ways it
still is, the presence of sizeable ethnic minorities means that we
are brought face to face with other religions.

2 Some pagan religions are evil and superstitious. But the great
world religions are worthy of respect, and their adherents often
practise them with more enthusiasm than some Christians
practise Christianity. It is utterly unreasonable, now that we can
observe them at first hand, to attribute these religions to the
work of the Devil.

3 It is commonly said that 'all religions say the same thing'. This
can now be seen to be false. Different world faiths have very different outlooks, beliefs, practices. These cannot all be true.

4 Christians believe that God revealed himself to the world
through a personal self-disclosure in Jesus Christ. This does not
exclude the possibility of other less-than-personal disclosures in
other faiths. The Divine Word, embodied in Jesus, can speak elsewhere. Divine grace is not to be constricted to that proportion of
the human race which is Christian.

5 Christians who are asked to share the richness of their own faith with members of other faiths must start from where these people are. They must first listen to them, and learn the riches of their inheritance and discern the hidden Christ within these faiths, and then tell them how, in their experience, the revealed Christ fulfils that which is lacking elsewhere.

6 Adherents of other faiths do not automatically go to hell. Such an idea is not compatible with a loving God, nor with the Scriptures. It is true that we can only know God fully as our heavenly Father through the Son ('No one comes to the Father except by me', John 14.6); but it is also true that 'God has no favourites, but that in every nation the man who is godfearing and does what is right is acceptable to him' (Acts 10.35).

7 Dialogue involves listening with respect and openness to what another has to say without in any way blunting one's own convictions. The following short summaries of great world faiths are most inadequate. Fuller descriptions are available from paperbacks or, better still, from their own adherents.

8 *Judaism (nearly half a million in UK)*

The Jewish Bible is the Old Testament. The written word is linked to oral tradition, which was itself later written down. Jews do not believe (as do Christians) that the Messiah has come: they await his coming before the End. The Jewish Law is revered by Jews, who are strict about its observance, especially food and Sabbath laws. Jews are firm monotheists, and they hold that their faith is not compatible with the Christian doctrine of the Trinity.

9 *Hinduism* (*500,000 in UK*)

This comprises the many religious beliefs and cults of India, many of great antiquity. Derived from Brahmanism, with its Trinity of Brahma, Vishnu and Siva, it ranges from lofty philosophy to crude mythology and superstition. The *Bhagavadgita* contains the most revered Holy Writings. Hindus are characterized by their acceptance of fate. The Hindu may accept all revelations as equal disclosures of Ultimate Reality: for them, Jesus is one of many 'Avatars'.

10 *Buddhism* (*about 50,000 in UK*)

The Buddha (Enlightened One) was a Nepalese Prince (born 563 BC) who left society to learn truth. Buddhism has five fundamental concepts: (i) all things are in a state of change; (ii) only the laws of change do not change; (iii) Karma is the law of spiritual and moral change – selfishness leads to suffering; (iv) Nirvana is salvation, the abolition of all egotism; (v) the truths of Buddhism are not derived from external authority but from personal experience. Some Buddhists believe in God, others do not.

11 *Islam* (*1.5 million in UK*)

Muhammad died in Arabia in AD 632. He wrote the Koran, the Muslim Scriptures. The Islamic creed is 'There is no God but Allah and Muhammad is his Prophet'. Islam reveres the Jewish patriarchs and respects Jesus as a prophet. Worship includes recital of the creed and set prayers, fasting in Ramadan, pilgrimage to Mecca. Ethics are often legalistic. There is a strong belief in an afterlife.

12 *Sikhism (200,000 in UK)*

Nanak (died AD 1539) founded Sikhism in India, a kind of reformed Hinduism. Three tenets are belief in God (the God of all men), the guru (holy man), Granth (the Sikh Scriptures). Chief differences from Christianity include transmigration of souls and predestination. The five Ks (so called from the Hindi words) introduced by Govind Guru Singh are: (i) uncut hair; (ii) short drawers; (iii) iron bangles; (iv) steel dagger; (v) comb (all still worn by the strict Sikh).

SECTS

13 In addition to other religions in this country, there are also semi-Christian sects, the largest of which are Mormons (185,000), Jehovah's Witnesses (150,000), Spiritualists (35,000) and the Church of Scientology (30,000). The 'Moonies' have gained notoriety and may have their charitable status removed.

14 The 'sects' give their adherents absolute certainty in a difficult and dangerous world. They generate strong feelings of 'belonging' and security, and often produce elements of fanaticism and world-weariness. They do not deserve the respect which Christians should accord the great world religions, although the sects have often concentrated on some aspects of Christianity which the mainstream churches have neglected.

NOTES

20

'One to Twelve'

1 *The ONE Name of Sure Salvation*

Jesus

2 *The TWO Great Commandments*

1 To love God with all I've got
2 To love my neighbour as myself

3 *The THREE Christian Virtues*

1 Faith
2 Hope
3 Charity

4 *The FOUR Cardinal Virtues*

1 Justice
2 Prudence
3 Temperance
4 Courage

5 *The FIVE Great Days*

1 Christmas Day
2 Good Friday

3   Easter Day
4   Whit Sunday
5   All Saints' Day

6   *The SIX Worst (Ultimate) Sins*

1   Presuming on God's mercy
2   Despair
3   Impugning a known good
4   Envy at another's good
5   Deliberate obstinacy in sin
6   Final impenitence

7   *The SEVEN Grave (Deadly) Sins and Their Opposites*

1   Pride (Humility)
2   Covetousness (Generosity)
3   Lust (Chastity)
4   Envy (Charity)
5   Greed (Temperance)
6   Anger (Patience)
7   Sloth (Diligence)

8   *The EIGHT Beatitudes*

Happy are:
1   The poor in spirit
2   Those who mourn
3   The meek
4   Those who hunger and thirst after righteousness
5   The merciful
6   The pure in heart
7   The peacemakers
8   Those who are persecuted for righteousness' sake

9 The NINE Ways of Sharing in Another's Sin

1 By advice
2 By command
3 By consent
4 By provocation
5 By praise or flattery
6 By concealment
7 By partaking
8 By silent acquiescence
9 By condonation

10 The TEN Commandments

1 Thou shalt have no other gods . . .
2 Thou shalt have no graven images
3 Thou shalt not take God's name in vain
4 Thou shalt keep holy the Sabbath day
5 Thou shalt honour thy father and mother
6 Thou shalt do no murder
7 Thou shalt not commit adultery
8 Thou shalt not steal
9 Thou shalt not bear false witness
10 Thou shalt not covet

11 ELEVEN Practical Works of Mercy

1 To feed the hungry and give drink to the thirsty
2 To clothe the destitute
3 To give shelter to the stranger and homeless
4 To visit those sick in mind or body
5 To visit and relieve the prisoners
6 To cheer the lonely and depressed
7 To help widows and orphans

8   To drive courteously and hospitably

9   To spend time listening to those in distress

10 To care for parents in their old age

11 To bury the dead

12 *TWELVE Subjects for Meditation and Prayer*

Remember, O Christian soul, that you have this day and every day:

1   God to glorify

2   Jesus to imitate

3   The Holy Spirit to recognize

4   A mind to exercise

5   A body to hallow

6   Forgiveness to receive

7   Time to use

8   Neighbours to love

9   Passions to moderate

10 Gentleness to learn

11 Perfection to attain

12 Heaven to hope for

NOTES

21

The Church

Can you be a Christian on your own?

1 Belonging is as important as believing. The Christian gospel is not the result of an individual's search for truth. It is 'good news' given to a group of people, shared by them with others, and handed on from generation to generation.

2 The Christian gospel therefore belongs to the whole Church of God. People share in it because they belong in some sense to that universal Church. It is always larger than any single person can comprehend.

3 Each individual tries to understand the Christian faith and to make it authentic for himself or herself.

4 Within the Church Christians share together their worship and life. Sharing is at the heart of Christianity. Solitary Christianity is a contradiction in terms. Without 'belonging' there is no authentic 'believing'.

What is the Church?

5 The Church is not a club of like-minded people. It consists rather of people of very different kinds, called together to be disciples of Christ.

6 Christians normally begin their membership of the Church at baptism. They meet together to be renewed in worship, united in Christ and sent into the world to serve their fellows.

7 Most people experience the Church through their local congregation. This is not just a local branch with a distant HQ. It is the local embodiment of the whole Church of God.

8 'Every member ministry' means that every member of the Church has some service to offer, whether in worship and prayer, or in sharing the gospel, or service to others.

9 The ordained ministry (the clergy) alone are authorized to the ministry of both word and sacrament. The Church is not here to serve the clergy: the clergy are ordained to serve the Church.

Is the Church perfect?

10 The Church, insofar as it is filled with God's Spirit, is divine in nature, and Scripture speaks of it as 'The Body of Christ', 'The Bride of Christ', 'The People of God'. At the same time it has a very human, institutional side, and is subject to human sin and failure. (In this it resembles individual Christian people.) One aspect of this is the division within the universal Church into churches and sects.

NOTES

22

The Church of England

1 There were Christians in England in the first (or second) century. The Church of England was refounded in AD 597 when St Augustine landed on the orders of Pope Gregory. A few years later St Aidan started missionary work in the north-east.

2 The Church of England has continued since then, until now. Up to the Reformation, all the Western Church was under the spiritual overlordship of the Pope.

3 The Reformation took place in different ways in different countries in Europe. In England it happened in three stages.

4 Henry VIII did not intend to alter the catholicity of the Church, but he did renounce the authority in England of the Bishop of Rome (the Pope), set up an English Bible in churches, and insisted that people should be taught the rudiments of their faith in English.

5 Under Edward VI, a new Prayer Book in English was introduced.

6 After the Roman Catholic Mary, Queen Elizabeth became Queen, and completed the Reformation of the Church of England. The Thirty-nine Articles set out the beliefs of the period (but they do not have binding force today). The Queen was excommunicated

by the Pope, and Roman Catholics were encouraged to attempt to overthrow her. The Queen took great care to see that episcopal succession was properly maintained.

7 The Book of Common Prayer was published in 1662. (It was revised in 1928, but this revision was not legalized.) New services in *Common Worship* are intended to be alternative, not substitute, services.

8 The Church of England is thus the continuance of the old Church, but reformed. It is both catholic and protestant; catholic in that it retains what is best in tradition, and protestant because it protests against what have been the errors of Rome, some (but not all) of which have been changed in the reforms of the Second Vatican Council near the end of the twentieth century.

9 The Church of England has the catholic Bible, the catholic sacraments of baptism and communion, the catholic ministry of bishops, priests and deacons, and the catholic creeds. The Church in Wales, the Church of Ireland and the Episcopal Church of Scotland are similar to the Church of England.

10 The intention of the Church of England is to be comprehensive. She includes liberals of the broad church (who concentrate on reason), people who are high church (tradition) and evangelicals (the Bible). All have a place within her, and all can worship the same Lord despite inevitable differences of belief. Charity should come first. She was intended to be the Church for all the people who live in this land. Although the Church of England has achieved a great deal of self-government it is (apart from its worship and doctrine) subject in the last resort to the state (e.g. although the Church selects names of people for a bishopric, the state actually makes the nomination).

Because the Church of England is still officially 'established' by law, it is the duty of the Church of England clergy to care for all who live within the boundaries of a parish.

11 The Church of England became, almost unintentionally, the Mother Church of a world-wide family of churches (known as the Anglican Communion, about 70 million), united by a common ethos and by communion with the Archbishop of Canterbury.

12 *The Roman Catholic Church: Chief Differences*

The Church of England does not believe in the infallibility of the Pope, nor in the 'Marian' dogmas. The Roman Catholic style of church government is more autocratic, with greater power vested in bishops and priests. In addition to doctrinal differences, there are ethical differences concerning contraception, abortion, remarriage, etc. Attempts at reunion with Anglicans faltered at the end of the twentieth century when the Church of England added to its disagreements with Rome the ordination of women; but although Anglicans and Roman Catholics are still divided and Anglicans cannot receive communion in their churches, they have grown much closer together, and more ways are being explored to grow closer.

13 *The Free Churches: Chief Differences*

The Church of England, unlike the Free Churches, has kept the threefold traditional ministry of bishop, priest and deacon, a fixed liturgy, the Church's calendar, and a certain amount of traditional ceremonial. The Free Churches chiefly comprise Methodists, Baptists and United Reformed (totalling 180 million world-wide). Although the Church of England turned down a Covenant with these Churches, she is in warm relationship with them and collaborates with them through CTBI (Churches

Together in Britain and Ireland). There is a renewed attempt to reunite with the Methodist Church.

14 *The Orthodox Churches: Chief Differences*

The Orthodox Churches have their ancestry in the ancient churches of the East. They hold to an earlier version of the creed ('the Holy Spirit . . . proceeding from the Father') and they generally disapprove of altering church tradition. Their public worship is characterized by chanting, and their spirituality includes reverence for icons. There are 189 million Orthodox Christians in the world. Relations between Anglicanism and the Orthodox Churches are very warm and the Church of England is in communion with some of them.

15 *The Ecumenical Movement* is an expression of the fact that churches generally are no longer in rivalry with one another, but seek to co-operate and learn from one another, believing that what they hold in common is far more important than what keeps them apart.

NOTES

23

Christian Responsibilities

1   There are very few absolute human rights. For example, we have
no absolute right to human happiness. If it is denied us, we can
grow into maturity through its lack. If it is given us, it is a gift
from God to be enjoyed.

2   *Our Body*

A person's body is 'a shrine of the indwelling Holy Spirit' (1
Corinthians 6.19); and so it should be treated with respect, kept
healthy and well groomed, and may be suitably embellished by
clothes, etc.; in a word, appropriately enjoyed.

3   *Our Mind*

A person's mind is part of his or her inheritance as a child of God
created in his image. By means of our mind we can distinguish
what is true from what is false, and what is right from what is
wrong. The mind too therefore should be kept healthy and well
groomed and its use appropriately enjoyed.

4   *Our Gifts*

Our talents are gifts from God, to be trained, used and enjoyed
by ourselves. Jesus never told us to despise our bodies or mind or
spirit. He told us to love our neighbours as ourselves (not more
than ourselves).

5 In order to be truly ourselves, we need to be able to receive from others what they want to give us and we need to give to others to help to meet their needs. This giving includes the giving of attention and time as well as practical service.

6 *Our Giving to the Church*

Some of our financial giving should be channelled towards the needs of the institutional Church, so that we may pay our proper share by way of membership. This is a direct and fairly quantifiable debt. It is not the same as helping those in need, or a sacrificial call to help some particular person or project to which we may feel we should respond.

7 *Almsgiving*

We need to give away a proportion of our money to those in need. Almsgiving is a primary duty, endorsed by Jesus. Some people give a tithe (10 per cent).

8 *Using Our Money*

We have a primary duty to those dependent on us to provide for them; and we may justifiably spend money on ourselves for holidays and modest pleasures, provided we also give to those in need.

9 Part of a Christian's giving is the passing on to others the gift of faith, for to keep it to oneself would be merely selfish.

10 All too often evangelism appears to the 'evangelized' as spiritual scalp-hunting, an attempt to impose on others our own views and experience. In reality, to pass on the gift of faith is not to smother other people but to let them be, not to tell them what

they need so much as to enable them to see for themselves what God wants to give them.

11 All forms of giving, to be authentic, require a personal self-awareness, the ability to receive and a respect for and sensitivity to others.

NOTES

24

Christian Behaviour

1   Jesus Christ is our role model for Christian behaviour.

2   Jesus taught us that there are two great commandments on which hang all Christian behaviour:

    (a)   to love God with all we've got;
    (b)   to love our neighbour as ourself.

3   We love God by worshipping him and by keeping his commandments in our dealings with others. We find these in the Ten Commandments (see Section 20).

4   We are to love ourselves, not in the sense of inflating our own importance or putting ourselves and our wishes in front of other people, but in the deeper sense of honouring our bodies, minds and spirits because we are children of God, and beloved by him. This gives us a proper sense of self-worth.

5   We are to love our neighbour in many ways. Here are some of them:

    (a)   by honouring others as people made in God's image;
    (b)   by kindness to others;
    (c)   by helping others in need, irrespective of class, colour or creed;

(d) by acts of service to others;

(e) by dealing justly with others, and seeking justice for them.

6 Christian behaviour is not only concerned with individuals: it is also concerned with corporate groups, in industry and commerce, and in local and national affairs. In these spheres the need for justice is predominant.

7 In considering the moral behaviour of any action we may take, we should distinguish (i) the nature of the act, (ii) the intention of the action, and (iii) the probable consequences of the action. Some acts are intrinsically wrong (e.g. murder). An intention to do something may be good, but the act itself may be wrong. An act is not moral just because its consequences are good. A combination of all three factors is needed.

8 It is not possible to give a blueprint of morality which covers all kinds of behaviour. We have to judge this for ourselves in the light of the principles above.

9 Jesus makes it clear in his teaching that Christians ought to go out of their way to help the poor, the underprivileged and those in need. We ought to look for the hidden Christ in others; as he taught 'anything you did for one of my brothers here, however humble, you did for me' (Matthew 25.40).

25

The Christian View of Sex and Marriage

1 Sexual reproduction originated, in the course of evolution, as the means of ensuring the best development of a species through combining the genes of both male and female, and through admixture of genes.

2 In human beings, with their unique ability to make personal relationships, sexual intercourse has become equally important as a means of exchanging mutual love and bonding.

3 The sexual instinct, in order to ensure the future of the human race, is very strong indeed. It therefore needs restraint, by law, custom and personal self-discipline, if it is to be properly used. (For example, this is why a person under the age of 16 cannot legally consent to intercourse.)

4 Because of its origins in human reproduction, men and women are mutually attracted to one another (heterosexuality). However, in a small minority of the population, some people are naturally attracted to members of their own sex (homosexuality, lesbianism).

5 There are some who have decided to remain single and to abstain from sexual intercourse for the sake of the gospel (celibacy), in

order to be more available to people in other ways. This state of life was recognized by Jesus (Matthew 19.12).

6   In order to ensure reproduction, nature has evolved in humans intense pleasure through sexual intercourse. However, to use intercourse simply as a source of pleasure is to trivialize it, since this negates its real function in reproduction and bonding.

7   Human beings who are deeply attracted to one another naturally feel an urge to engage in sexual intercourse. Christian teaching requires that this should be reserved for a permanent partnership; and this for good reasons:

   (a) it is only within such a partnership that children should be brought into the world, for they need this kind of security as they grow up;
   (b) sexual intercourse properly involves self-giving without reserve, which can only take place within a permanent partnership.

8   The Church of England approves of the use of contraceptives as a responsible way of limiting the number of children in a family, while at the same time welcoming intercourse (in marriage) as a means of exchanging love and increasing bonding.

9   Some couples have difficulty in the reproduction of children. For them modern science and technology have evolved means of reproduction which do not involve sexual intercourse (e.g. *in vitro* fertilization) as a means of overcoming this problem. Some of these methods may cause moral problems.

10 Many couples today live together without being married. They may have varying degrees of commitment, in some cases equal to

those of marriage. Jesus was a guest at a wedding (John 2.1ff.) and he spoke unambiguously in favour of marriage. 'God made them male and female. For this reason a man shall leave his father and mother and be made one with his wife; and the two shall become one flesh' (Mark 10.6f.). There are good reasons for marriage rather than cohabitation:

(a) Marriages have been shown to last longer than unmarried cohabitation.
(b) At a wedding a couple strengthen their commitment by openly pledging lasting love and faithfulness to each other.
(c) A wedding is a public statement to the community that a couple intend to live in lifelong partnership.
(d) Marriage fulfils for both partners a deep psychological need.

11 In marriage, lifelong partnership is promised by husband and wife. In their choice of partner, more is required than mere sexual attraction, which can fade. So sadly some marriages die. Jesus is reported to have disapproved of remarriage (Mark 10.11) but when a marriage has died, even though it may seem to contradict his teaching, it may be in the best interest of both the former partners not to stay single and celibate.

12 Marriage 'is a gift of God in creation and a means of his grace' (Marriage Service). There is a very great blessing in a happy marriage, which is a school of love, mirroring the love of Christ for his Church and giving a foretaste of the mutual love that awaits us in heaven.

26

Some Basic Christian Texts (RSV)

1 *Initiative Towards God*

'Ask, and it will be given you; seek, and you will find; knock, and it will be opened to you' (Matthew 7.7).

2 *Openness and Acceptance*

'Truly, I say to you, whoever does not receive the kingdom of God like a child shall not enter it' (Mark 10.15).

3 *The Right Priorities*

'Do not be anxious about your life' (Matthew 6.25). 'Seek first his kingdom and his righteousness' (Matthew 6.33).

4 *Stammering Faith*

'Lord, I believe: help my unbelief' (Mark 9.24).

5 *Love*

'There is no fear in love, but perfect love casts out fear' (1 John 4.18).

6 *Simplicity*

'We brought nothing into the world, and we cannot take anything out of the world; but if we have food and clothing, with these we shall be content' (1 Timothy 6.7, 8).

7 *Pursuit of Truth*

'Sanctify them in the truth; thy word is truth' (John 17.17). 'The truth will make you free' (John 8.32).

8 *Reversal of Worldly Values*

'Whoever would save his life will lose it; and whoever loses his life for my sake and the gospel's will save it' (Mark 8.35). 'Many that are first will be last, and the last first' (Mark 10.31).

9 *Guilt*

'We shall know that we are of the truth, and reassure our hearts before him whenever our hearts condemn us; for God is greater than our hearts, and he knows everything' (1 John 3.19, 20).

10 *Readiness to Take Action*

'Not every one who says to me, "Lord, Lord," shall enter the kingdom of heaven, but he who does the will of my Father who is in heaven' (Matthew 7.21).

11 *Forgiveness*

'Repay no one evil for evil, but take thought for what is noble in the sight of all. If possible, so far as it depends upon you, live peaceably with all' (Romans 12.17, 18).

12 *Hope*

'Here we have no lasting city, but we seek the city which is to
come' (Hebrews 13.14).

NOTES

NOTES

NOTES

NOTES